The Ballantine House

The Ballantine House
and the
Decorative Arts Galleries
at The Newark Museum

Ulysses Grant Dietz

The Ballantine House presentation of The Newark Museum's permanent collection of decorative arts in the exhibition *House & Home*, this publication and related public programs are made possible through the Lila Wallace-Reader's Digest Fund Museum Collections Accessibility Initiative.

THE NEWARK MUSEUM, NEW JERSEY 1994

The Ballantine House presentation of The Newark Museum's permanent collection of decorative arts
in the exhibition *House & Home*, this publication and related public programs are made possible through the
Lila Wallace-Reader's Digest Fund Museum Collections Accessibility Initiative.

Other major capital funding for the restoration of the Ballantine House was contributed from
City of Newark Capital Projects, New Jersey Historic Trust, National Endowment for the Humanities,
National Endowment for the Arts and other foundations, corporate and private support.

The Newark Museum receives operating support from City of Newark and State of New Jersey,
The New Jersey State Council on the Arts/Department of State and Essex County.
Funding for acquisitions and activities other than operations must be developed from outside sources.

ISBN 0-932828-30-2

Cover
The Master Bedroom of the Ballantine House

Title Spread
The Ballantine House Window, an allegory of the family name,
which in Gaelic means "Fire Worshiper." It is attributed to Tiffany Studios.

Contemporary Period Photographs
Justin Van Soest, New York

Stained Glass Photographs
Shelly Kusnetz

Contemporary Exterior Photographs
Armen Photographers

Decorative Arts Object Photographs
Sarah Wells

Period Photographs
Pages 11, 12 collection of Newark Public Library

All Other Photographs
The Newark Museum Archives

Design
Milton Simpson, Johnson & Simpson Graphic Designers, New Jersey

Printing
Herlin Press, Inc., Connecticut

This book is printed on acid and chlorine free, pre-and post-consumer recycled paper stock.

Foreword

The Ballantine House holds a unique place, not only in New Jersey, but in the entire New York metropolitan area. Although New York, Connecticut and New Jersey now can boast of a wide assortment of Victorian villas and cottages, mansions and manor houses, Newark's own Ballantine House is the only extant urban mansion in the region that is authentically restored and open to the public.

Its restoration is a tribute to many individuals and to an institution that early on came to recognize the value of late-nineteenth century decorative arts. The Ballantine House was acquired by The Newark Museum in 1937, and fortunately preserved intact until the mid-1970s, when my predecessor, Samuel C. Miller, and the Trustees spearheaded the effort to open the first floor to the public, restored to its turn-of-the-century grandeur. The House was subsequently designated a National Historic Landmark and won acclaim as one of the finest nineteenth-century period restorations in the country.

The present restoration, an entire revamping of all crucial mechanical systems as well as aesthetic embellishments to second floor period rooms, has been accomplished through the efforts of the Trustee fundraising committee under the directorship of Chairman and President Kevin Shanley, and ably headed by Lois Lautenberg. The Trustee Building Committee, chaired by Richard F. Blanchard, provided oversight for this intricate construction project. Ulysses Grant Dietz, Curator of Decorative Arts, along with a team of educators, exhibition designers and scholars, has provided a lavish reinstallation and a thoughtful reinterpretation.

Funding from the Lila Wallace-Reader's Digest Fund Museum Collections Accessibility Initiative made possible our expanded interpretation of how this one house embodied a particular concept of home and family life. The Newark Museum is especially proud to have made a commitment, with the backing of this Fund, to expand our audience for the decorative arts through this new interpretation. It has been very gratifying to work with our collections in shaping the reinstallation of the Ballantine House and the *House & Home* exhibition.

We are equally grateful to City of Newark Capital Projects, the New Jersey Historic Trust, the National Endowment for the Humanities, the National Endowment for the Arts and the many individuals, corporations and foundations who have made it possible to restore the fabric of the Ballantine House and preserve it into the next century.

Since it first opened in 1976, the Ballantine House has become one of The Newark Museum's most beloved aspects. The reopening of this house symbolized Newark's nineteenth-century prominence as a great industrial city and serves as a metaphor for Newark's renaissance at the turn of this century.

As you enter through the massive oak door beneath the grand staircase of the Ballantine House, you enter another world and time. The restoration, climate control and complete reinterpretation of the Ballantine House have transformed it into something that is both very familiar and entirely new. The Ballantine House now provides an educational — and, I hope, emotional — experience available in very few places across the country.

Mary Sue Sweeney Price
Director

Acknowledgments

To properly thank everyone who was part of the Ballantine House project really means thanking literally *every* person in this Museum, even those not directly involved.

From the very beginning of the Ballantine House/*House & Home* project, I have been fortunate to work with my Director, Mary Sue Sweeney Price, who has been both cheerleader and conscience throughout this lengthy process. She and her deputy directors, Ward Mintz and Rena Zurofsky, have each shouldered great responsibility and have worked hard to make the Ballantine House a reality. From the time the restoration and reinterpretation of the house was first conceived, I have had an exhibition team working with me—Lucy Brotman, Susan Newberry, and Tim Wintemberg. Together we have gone places where none of us had ever gone before, and have learned to look at the Ballantine House and the decorative arts collection in a new way.

All of this would not have been possible without the generous support of the Lila Wallace-Reader's Digest Fund Museum Collections Accessibility Initiative. In addition to capital monies, the Fund made it possible to bring in our great team of interpretive consultants, Michael Ettema, Clement Alexander Price, James Sims, and Gretchen Sullivan Sorin, who worked with the "home team" in formulating a dramatic new script for the House. Michael Graves designed the beautiful new galleries within the century-old structure, providing the perfect architectural connection with the rest of the Museum complex. Joseph Sullivan served as the Graves office's Project Architect for the Ballantine House.

Special thanks are due to the Museum's Trustees and staff who worked so hard on all the fundraising efforts that helped us reach our $4 million goal for the Ballantine House project. Kevin Shanley, our Chairman, worked with the Chair of the Campaign for the Ballantine House, Lois Lautenberg, and all the members of the fundraising committee. Peggy Dougherty, Marysue DePaola, and Brian Ferriso coordinated the fundraising efforts at the Museum. Business Administrator Dominic Lisanti ably handled our funding.

David Palmer coordinated the entire complex design aspect of the Ballantine House/*House & Home* project, juggling many different aspects of the exhibition and the historic restoration. The John O'Hara Company undertook the sensitive construction project, with Frank Lemire acting as construction manager. Frank treated the Ballantine House with the same care as if it was his own home, ably assisted by Olav Brastad as construction superintendent. Building Conservation Associates monitored the conservation of the historic fabric of the house, with Claudia Kavenagh spending many hours on site. Claudia, Frank and Olav not only helped us treat the house in the best possible way from a preservation standpoint, they also made discoveries that gave us new insight into the house's decoration and construction.

Richard Heaps, collections manager, along with Brenna Manuel and Johanna McClelland, masterminded the cleaning, inventory and moving of hundreds of objects, from matchboxes to marble statuary. They were assisted by willing volunteers, Fredrick Branch, Mimi Cohen, Sue Goldberg, and Carl Szego, who washed linens, hung draperies, polished silver, vacuumed upholstery, dusted books, and cleaned furniture with cotton swabs and distilled water. Fredrick Branch also built the exquisite scale model of the house for the Orientation Gallery.

I am particularly grateful for the help of the exhibition staff, who placed finishing touches on the exhibition and installation, taking time from other projects to attend to mine: Roger Brooks, Robert Coates, David Miller, and Daniel Schnur. The heaviest work in the House would never have been accomplished without the assistance of Bill Bloodgood and his staff. I thank Ellis Clark, Bernard Graham, David Hudley, Clifford Lewis, John Maya, James Mazza, Bernard McKinley, Eugene Nichols, Atta Owusu, Andrew Parr, Edmond Phillips, Edivurgo Reyes, Hector Rodriguez, Wayne Ross, Darrell Townsend, Gerald Williams, and Silas Worth for all their invaluable help.

Lucy Brotman coordinated the difficult job of acquiring appropriate photographic and historical material for the exhibition, and Margaret DiSalvi coordinated the extensive photography required for this book. Susan Newberry worked with Newark City Historian, Charles Cummings, in the Newark Public Library's vast photographic collections, and the Museum's researchers, Michelle Clanton, Leslie Littel, and Gwen Motley scoured the entire country for appropriate images. Marilyn Fish and Margaret Gaertner assisted me greatly in researching historical decorating details relative to the billiard room and bedrooms. Justin Van Soest, Shelly Kusnetz, Sarah Wells, and Armen Shamlian are responsible for the wonderful new photographs used in the exhibition and in this volume. Superb editing was provided by Sheila Schwartz, and handsome graphic design by Milton Simpson.

The Museum volunteer docents, headed by their special Ballantine House committee, Virginia Barlage, Anne Cummings, Doris Froehlich, Nicki Kessler, Patsy Nance and Marian Soloway, have studied and read enormous amounts of material in order to be prepared to help visitors appreciate and understand the "new" Ballantine House and its galleries. Likewise, the Education Department's Alejandro Ramirez and Benita Wolffe have worked with Helene Konkus and her Lending Collection staff to prepare extensive teaching materials for the Museum instructors to use in preparing their school programs for the house.

Diane Zediker did a great job working with Pat Faison and Keshia Townes to coordinate the publicity campaign. Barbara Lowell and Kristine Hood in the membership office have developed a membership campaign to entice new members to come and see the Ballantine House/*House & Home* galleries. Ruth Barnet, the curatorial secretary, kept track of my whereabouts and assisted with the manuscript of this publication.

Andrew Zietarski kept close watch on the many complicated aspects of operations and security, from monitoring the newly-installed climate control systems to coordinating maintenance help and attendants for the house. Additionally, he and his security staff, Ellie Cooper, Franklin Cooper, Margaret Jenkins, Errol Mullings, James Malone, Kim Sampson and Jimmy Smith, kept track of our comings and goings, and unlocked the doors for the many people who needed access to the house.

Finally I'd like to thank Samuel C. Miller, my first boss, whose own foresight and love of the Ballantine House were responsible for saving it in the first place. One of the highlights of this project was taking him to see for the first time the master bedroom, his office for twenty-one years, restored to its Victorian glory.

To all of these people I give my heartfelt thanks. And to the visitors to the Ballantine House, both old friends and new, I bid you welcome, one and all.

Ulysses Grant Dietz
Curator, Decorative Arts
Project Director

The Ballantine House and the Decorative Arts Galleries at The Newark Museum

W hen John and Jeannette Ballantine built their big brick house on the fashionable upper end of Newark's Washington Street in 1885, it was intended to be as much a symbol of who they were as it was a home in which to continue to raise their half-grown family. Today it remains a symbol, even more powerful than a century ago. For the Ballantine House stands as a rare survivor, an emissary from a Victorian world as lost to us as that of the dinosaurs.

THE ROBERT AND
JOHN BALLANTINE HOUSES, 1892,
WASHINGTON PARK, NEWARK

When the Ballantines' new house stood basking in the October sun in the fall of 1885, it symbolized to the family all that was good about the great City of Newark. With its deep orange-pink brick and crisp gray limestone, its tall plate-glass windows reflecting the trees in Washington Park, the house was a symbol of the city's commercial power, made possible by its industrialists and its diverse immigrant population. Irish, German, and Italian families had been coming to Newark since the 1830s, drawn by its reputation as a city where a poor man could strike it rich with hard work and the right kind of luck. The Ballantine mansion was built, literally and figuratively, by the hard work of these new Americans. The family's own great fortune was newly founded on Newark's national importance as a transportation hub, and, as second-generation Newarkers, they basked in the comfort and cultivation of the city's growing prosperity. The Ballantine House, and the family that lived in it, stood in a green oasis in the heart of a thriving metropolis and looked complacently toward the coming century.

DINING ROOM PRE-RESTORATION, 1970s

Today, over a century later, the house remains on Washington Street, its glittering windows still reflecting the trees in the park. It continues to symbolize what is great about Newark—a city with a sense of its own remarkable history, and an understanding of its complicated social and industrial heritage. As in the late nineteenth century, a large proportion of Newark's citizens were not born in this country, and its neighborhoods reflect a similar ethnic and racial diversity. But upper Washington Street is commercial now, no longer a fashionable residential enclave—nor has it been so since the early 1920s. Gone are the Vanderpools, the Frelinghuysens, the Scudders, and the Wards, and gone are the fine houses that once surrounded the park and set the tone for the city's elite. The Ballantine House stands alone today, dwarfed by office buildings, and even by the Museum next door. Where once it stood tall and grandiose amidst its neighbors, today it nestles more humbly among the towers of a very different Newark.

The survival of the Ballantine House is in some ways a miracle, and is of unparalleled importance for the people of New Jersey. New Jersey is a state of suburbs, with a vast population of suburbanites who have forgotten Newark's grandeur and importance in the history of the American city. New Jersey is also a state of urbanites, most of whom have never known their home cities as rich and brimming with an unbridled optimism shared by all residents. The American dream was born in New Jersey's cities in the nineteenth century, and the Ballantine House stands as a living symbol of one family's dream come true.

Completed in 1885, the house was lived in by three generations of the Ballantine family, but only during the lifetime of Mrs. Ballantine. John and Jeannette Ballantine were a middle-aged couple with four children when they moved into their new home. Alice, their only daughter, was persuaded to stay on and raise her own family here, so that Mrs. Ballantine would not be left alone in her widowhood. But in 1919, at Mrs. Ballantine's death, the house was sold by her children to the Commercial Casualty Insurance Company. Washington Park, so called since the eighteenth century, was rapidly being overwhelmed by the city's prosperity, and commercial buildings were rising, destroying the neighborhood's oasis-like atmosphere. Alice Ballantine Young, along with

many of her peers, moved her family to a new house in Forest Hill, a remote northern part of the city that was just being developed as a fashionable suburb.

The insurance company treated the house with surprising gentleness, apparently understanding its importance as a landmark in the city's history. A long brick office wing was appended to the back of the house in two phases, first in 1922 and then in 1926. The old kitchen and the servants' rooms above it were eliminated, and all but one of the original family bathrooms were removed. The old butler's pantry was converted to two modern lavatories, and the sole remaining bathroom on the second floor was likewise modernized. A small dumbwaiter was installed to carry heavy documents to the basement storerooms. An enormous coal-burning furnace was added to heat the new buildings. Great care was taken to preserve the original woodwork, fireplaces, and plaster moldings throughout the house; heavy industrial linoleum was rolled out over the original floorboards. Modern lighting fixtures were installed, but otherwise the house remained intact.

The Newark Museum Association built its new building at 49 Washington Street in 1925, on the site of the eighteenth-century Marcus L. Ward House. The Museum acquired the Ballantine House and its office building in 1937. A small umbilical connection was made between the first floors and basements of the Museum building and the insurance company. Dorothy (Mrs. George) McNally, was put in charge of moving the Museum staff into its spacious new offices. Even long after her retirement as assistant to the Director in 1983, Mrs. McNally continued her involvement in the ongoing saga of the house.

The Museum did not originally have any clear plan to restore the house, but simply wanted the space it afforded. For this reason, the Museum left the house itself virtually untouched during the next thirty-five years. Victorian buildings were not valued in this country in the 1930s and 1940s, and many fell to the wrecker's ball. Early plans to raze the house and expand the Museum to the north were cut short by America's entry into World War II, and thus the house survived another historic hurdle.

In the late 1960s plans were again afoot to demolish the house, which was seen simply as a white elephant. A young, and then unknown, architect from Princeton named Michael Graves was called in to design the new Museum addition. Ironically, the office wing from the 1920s was to be spared, because its uncluttered commercial space was desirable. But Newark's bad luck turned into the house's good luck, and the turmoil and financial problems of the late sixties once again held off the wrecker's ball. Plans for the Museum's expansion were postponed, and the house continued on in its capacity as an office building.

In the early 1970s, as a memorial to his first wife, Nell Schoellkopf Ely Miller, Museum Director Samuel C. Miller oversaw the restoration of Alice Ballantine Young's third-floor library as the Trustees' Room. Thus the fate of the house was sealed, and its long-term preservation assured.

The first restoration of the house began in earnest in 1975, with a grant from the City of Newark Capital Projects and private funders, and for the national Bicentennial in 1976 the Ballantine House opened its doors to the public for the first time. With the support of the city and of private donors, four main first-floor rooms and the entrance hallway were restored to reflect the Ballantine family's residence in the 1880s and 1890s. In 1985 the United States Department of the Interior named the Ballantine House a National Historic Landmark, the highest honor accorded to a historic structure in this country.

With the completion of first phases of The Newark Museum's Master Plan in 1989, all staff offices were moved out of the second floor of the Ballantine House, and the full restoration project commenced. The Museum's Master Plan architect, Michael Graves, still a professor at Princeton, but now internationally celebrated for his distinctive architectural style, agreed to take on the job of project architect. Working with the Director, the Curator of Decorative Arts, the Education Department, and the Exhibitions Department, the Graves office began work in 1992. The goal was to transform this unique survivor of Newark's industrial heyday into a state-of-the-art museum house, incorporating period rooms and exhibition galleries, and integrating the Victorian structure with the overall Museum complex. This volume is the document of that project.

The Ballantine Family and the City of Newark

Wh" hen Peter Ballantine immigrated to the United States in 1820, he could hardly have imagined that eighty-five years later the brewery he established in Newark would be referred to as "one of the oldest and most celebrated in the country." Born in Mauchline, Ayrshire, Scotland, on November 16, 1791, Ballantine was a poor man looking for a fresh start in America. He first took a job in a tavern in Black Rock, Connecticut, later moving to Troy, New York. He learned about the brewing business in the mid-1820s while employed in a Troy ale brewery. In 1830, at age thirty-eight, finding himself

A BALLANTINE BREWERY WAGON, CIRCA 1885

prosperous enough to settle down, he married Julia Wilson (1796-1868) of Troy. Frank Urquart, in his 1913 A History of the City of Newark, New Jersey, said, "Thrifty and canny...he soon found himself with sufficient capital to start his own brewing plant and to settle down with his bride in a home of his own." By 1831, Peter and Julia had moved to Albany, New York, where their three sons were born—Peter Hood (1831-1882), John Holme (1834-1895), and Robert F. (1836-1905). Ballantine is listed in the 1832-1840 Albany City Directories as a brewer, first on North Market Street, and later, between 1838 and 1840, at 14 Lansing Street. By 1838, another Scottish immigrant, Thomas McCredie,

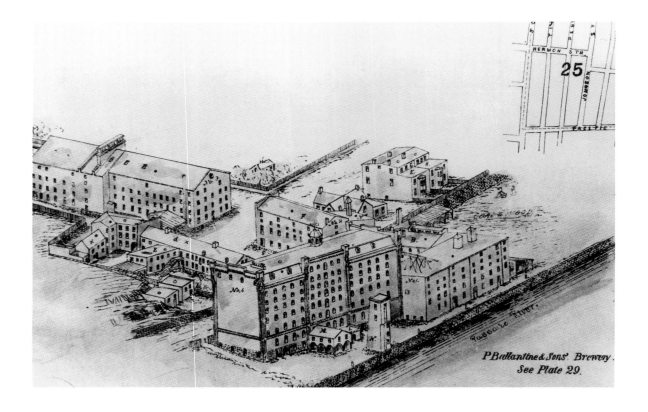

arrived in Albany, and he "soon made the acquaintance of Peter Ballantine, a brother Scotsman, the famous maltster and brewer."

Like many other entrepreneurs in the post-depression year of 1840, Peter Ballantine reckoned that the New York City area, with its enormous population, offered greater business potential than Albany. Only nine miles from New York City, Newark was at that time known for its abundant supply of fresh water, and Peter Ballantine moved his young family to Newark in 1840, leasing the eighteenth-century stone house at 36 Broad Street owned by Colonel John I. Plume (now the rectory of the Episcopal House of Prayer).

Peter Ballantine formed a partnership with Erastus Patterson, and was listed in the 1841-1842 Newark City Directory as a brewer at 514 High Street. The partners bought a brewery, which stood on the west side of the street between Orange and James Streets (behind the present-day Rutgers University Law School) and had been established in 1805 by General John M. Cummings. After passing through several owners, the brewery was leased in 1840 to Patterson and Ballantine by Thomas Morton. The partnership continued until 1847, when Patterson moved to New York City and Ballantine acquired sole ownership of the brewery. By 1848, Ballantine had opened a retail sales office at 134 Cedar Street, New York, and had purchased a large tract of land on Front Street and the Passaic River, Newark, where he constructed a new ale brewery.

As was still customary in the first half of the nineteenth century, a manufacturer lived as close as possible to his shop or factory. Peter and Julia built a small stucco house near the brewery, where they lived from 1849 until his death in 1883. By the time of Peter Ballantine's death, according to Urquart's 1913 history, "the huge factory buildings had begun to close in on the little house and to spread over the grassy lawns about it." Peter and Julia's sons had already moved to more fashionable parts of Newark. After Peter's death, the brewmaster's house was occupied by the superintendent of the plant, who took over the role of caretaker of the vast brewery.

During the 1850s, Ballantine built a second brewery adjacent to the first malt house. This new brewery had a capacity of 100 barrels of ale per day and, as sales increased, Ballantine was required to brew twice a day instead of four times a week. According to J.L. Bishop's *The History of American Manufacture* (1866), the first Ballantine malt house and brewery had a 30,000 bushel capacity. Two additional malt houses, erected in 1866, increased the storage capacity to 190,000 bushels of malt. By 1867, the brewery was producing 36,500 barrels of ale per year. By 1913, this figure had skyrocketed to over 500,000 barrels. In 1874, Ballantine employed 175 workers, and by 1915 that number had increased to 1,800.

Brewing was one of the many industries that resulted in Newark's designation in 1877 as "the third city of the Union in manufacturing importance." Beginning in the 1840s, Newark started its rise as a major industrial center, leading in the production of such commodities as rubber, soap, beer, thread, glue, leather goods, trunks, shoes, hats, silver, jewelry, cutlery, tobacco products, varnish, and fertilizer. In 1849 it was said of Newark:

> People appear to be flocking from every direction to share with us the luxury of living
> in so pleasant and beautiful a city as Newark, where anyone who is willing to work
> can earn enough to make both ends meet, and have something left over at the end of
> the year, if economy is exercised.

The rapid industrialization of Newark can be dramatically seen in the expanding population: 17,202 in 1840 when Peter and Julia brought their family here; 105,059 in 1870. Peter was among the first wave of foreign-born immigrants to come to Newark, along with Irish Catholics and Germans (both Jewish and Christian), who began to arrive in the 1830s. They were followed by Italians, starting in the 1860s, and then by Eastern Europeans, again both Jewish and Christian, in the 1880s. Newark, with its towering smokestacks, growing labor force, busy harbor, and bustling streets, was truly a land of opportunity in the Victorian era. It far exceeded all other New Jersey cities in terms of size, population, and wealth. Newark became the center of the state's insurance, banking, and retail business.

Securely positioned in the midst of this boomtown was the Ballantine family and its brewery. William F. Ford, in *The Industrial Interests of Newark, New Jersey* (1874), provides a description of the brewery, calling it:

> *admirable for facilitating business, having a fine frontage on the Passaic River,*
> *so that grain, coals, and other material can be received or shipped with great*
> *convenience. The buildings cover about five acres of ground, and are provided*
> *with the most improved machinery and arrangements. The brewery proper is five*
> *stories high and measures 80 feet x 150 feet, with an additional wing 65 feet*
> *square. The principal malt house is eight stories in height, and measures*
> *75 feet x 175 feet. As one approaches Newark from New York, by rail or river,*
> *this establishment is perhaps the most prominent object in view.*

The firm was listed in the Newark City Directory as "P. Ballantine" until 1857, when it became "P. Ballantine & Sons." The partnership of Peter and his three sons continued until his death in 1883, at which time the company was incorporated. In 1868, with a change in city street numbers, the brewery's address became 78-110 Front Street. By 1871, a new and larger brewery was necessary. Mr. Ballantine's office and sales room were built at the end of Fulton Street.

Until 1879, the Ballantine brewery brewed only ale, but Peter's eldest son, Peter Hood, urged his father to expand, and the company bought out the bankrupt Schalk Brewery on Freeman Street. Here Ballantine began to brew lager beer, under the name "Ballantine & Company," to distinguish it from the ale brewery. The huge success of the Ballantine breweries was directly due to the city's large population of newly immigrated Europeans, with whom the rich, heavy lager beer found a ready market. The familiar Ballantine trademark of the interlocking three rings—signifying purity, strength, and flavor—was also adopted in 1879.

The brewing industry increased with such volume that Newark became a national production center, exporting beer throughout the United States. With his ultramodern brew houses, malt houses, and bottling works, Peter Ballantine easily outproduced the other members of Newark's "Big Five" of brewing: Joseph Hensler (founded 1860), Gottfried Krueger (founded 1865), Christian Feigenspan (founded 1875), and George Weidenmeyer (founded 1879).

In addition to nationwide distribution, local delivery of Ballantine ale and beer required a stable of 255 horses and a fleet of more than 100 wagons. The massive brewery stable complex backed up to the Frelinghuysen estate on Park Place, on the east side of Military Park, the Colonial militia ground.

Peter Hood Ballantine, the eldest son, died in 1882 at the age of fifty. He was survived by his wife, Isabelle Linen Ballantine (1835-1911), and four children: Sara, George, Isabel, and Mary. His father died, aged ninety-two, the following year. On June 30, 1883, after the founder's death, a corporation was established with John Holme Ballantine as president and Robert F. Ballantine as vice president. After John's death in 1895, Robert Ballantine served as president of the brewery until his death in 1905. During Robert Ballantine's tenure as president, a new bottling plant was built and liquid malt, known as cereal syrup, was manufactured. In addition to its use by brewers, liquid malt was also used by bakeries and laundries (liquid malt production helped the brewery survive Prohibition).

By 1900 the Ballantine brewery covered twelve acres. The ale brewery, malt houses, and elevator were situated on Front, Fulton, and Rector Streets. The lager beer brewery and bottling plant were bordered by Freeman, Christie, Oxford, Ferry, and Bowery Streets.

After Robert Ballantine's death in 1905, the brewery underwent another reorganization, and for the first time since 1840 the Ballantine name was not represented in the company's management. While the financial crash of 1929 and Prohibition made encroachments on the volume and output of the brewery, it never affected the financial solvency of the company.

On June 1, 1933, the entire stock of P. Ballantine & Sons was sold and transferred to an investment group headed by Carl W. Badenhausen. After ninety-three years, control of the foremost American brewery passed from the Ballantine family.

WASHINGTON PARK, CIRCA 1900

JOHN AND

JEANNETTE BALLANTINE,

CIRCA 1885

The Ballantines
and Washington Park

Designated as one of the three public open spaces when the city was founded in 1666, Washington Park, known in Colonial times as the Market Square, traditionally provided a quiet interlude from the bustling downtown traffic. Since the eighteenth century, Newark families had built houses on the park, and by the 1860s and 1870s Washington Park was considered one of Newark's most fashionable neighborhoods. Within the brick and clapboard houses that surrounded the park resided many of Newark's oldest families.

In the 1880s, both of Newark's uptown parks, Washington and Military Park, were residential oases—quiet, green retreats from the bustling crowds, carriages, and trolleys of the "Four Corners," the downtown crossing of Broad and Market Streets. Even though Washington Park was not, by modern standards, far away from downtown, it was psychologically isolated by its residential nature. Regardless of the enormous Ballantine brewery looming just a few blocks east of the park, it was, in the minds of its residents, a quiet haven in which to raise their families.

Peter Ballantine's traditional ideas had given way to those of a younger generation, and this generation did not want to live too near its place of business. In the spirit of the Victorian era, residential neighborhoods (for those who could afford it) provided an antidote to the dirt, the noise, and the danger of city life, while still convenient to the attractions of a busy commercial and cultural center.

In 1878, John H. Ballantine purchased the property at 43 Washington Street and moved his wife, Jeannette Boyd (1836-1919), and four children from their home near the brewery at 70 Front Street. In 1879, John's younger brother, Robert, purchased the adjacent stucco house at 37 Washington Street, formerly the home of William and Catherine Faitoute.

With the death of his father and elder brother, John Ballantine became president in 1883 of one of the largest breweries in the world. He immediately began plans for a town house suitable to his new position. During the Colonial era and early nineteenth century, rich families had identified themselves by building fine houses, but during the Victorian era the house had become an even more powerful symbol, not just of economic status, but of American progress. Before the Civil War, the American house had become the American Home, embodying an ideal of domestic comfort, convenience, and cultivation that was seen as unique to American democracy. Throughout the nineteenth century, as industry expanded and more goods were produced, increasing numbers of Americans were able to build and own their own homes. People whose grandparents had never considered owning a home were now homeowners. Those who, like the Ballantines, were lucky enough to be at the top of the economic ladder were expected to build houses that expressed the highest achievement of the "ideal" home. A fine home was not just a status symbol, it was a patriotic duty.

To create his family's ideal home, John Ballantine purchased an additional lot at 47 Washington Street from Joseph Ward and hired the services of architect George Edward Harney, A.I.A. (1840-1924). Ballantine called for the razing of the two existing houses, neither of them very old, and the building of a new house. During the two-year period 1883-1885, while the house was being constructed, the Ballantine family moved into the former home of Episcopal Bishop Thomas A. Starkey at 53 Washington Street, built in 1857 by Edwin Van Antwerp (and now the site of The Newark Museum's South Wing).

Harney, best known for his book on barns and stables (Barns, Outbuildings and Fences, 1870), designed numerous residential and commercial buildings in the New York area in the 1870s and 1880s, including the Col. William Roebling House in Trenton, the Mercantile Library, and the old Brooks Brothers building in New York, and St. Mary's Church in Cold Spring Harbor, New York. Born in Lynn, Massachusetts, Harney studied with noted nineteenth-century American architect Alonzo Lewis. By 1863, Harney was an established architect, and had offices in both Cold Spring and Newburgh, New York. The Ballantine House is one of his few surviving buildings. Harney also designed the large brick carriage house which still stands at the west end of the Ballantine property, where it opened onto Plane Street (now University Avenue).

Harney's plans for John and Jeannette Ballantine consisted of a twenty-seven-room, three-story structure with a full basement and attic. It was built of pink-orange Philadelphia pressed brick and trimmed with gray Wyoming sandstone. Although nominally in the Renaissance style, inspired by the urban Italian palazzi of the sixteenth century, the house was truly eclectic, in an era when variety was an essential feature of good "modern" taste.

THE VAN ANTWERP/STARKEY HOUSE

[DEMOLISHED 1911]

THE THREE HOUSES

ON WASHINGTON PARK,

THAT THE BALLANTINE FAMILY

BOUGHT CIRCA 1875

THE BALLANTINE HOUSE FROM WASHINGTON PARK, 1886

When the Ballantine family moved into its grand new house in the fall of 1885, they proudly had photographs taken of the interiors. Three of these pictures—the library, parlor, and reception room—survive, and were used in the 1976 restoration, providing priceless evidence of the original look of the rooms. The reception room shows two high-backed reception chairs dating to the 1850s (and from Newark's Jelliff & Co.) and clearly brought with the family from its old house. These chairs were freshly upholstered for the new house. The bronze and marble candelabra on the mantelpiece, as well as the original andirons, are now part of the Museum's collections, and have been used in the restoration.

In the parlor (which was called the drawing room by the decorators, but the parlor by the architect), the silvered bronze sconces, fender, and andirons survive, as do the elaborate ormolu and enamel clock and candelabra from the mantelpiece.

Although not visible in the picture, the original cherry fall-front desk survives from the library, and stands where it was placed in 1885. Of the three rooms—library, parlor, and reception room—only the library remained unchanged until Mrs. Ballantine's death.

In 1891, a major redecoration was undertaken of the entrance hall, reception room, parlor, and music room. It is not clear just why this was done, but one possibility is that this was the year Alice turned seventeen, and would probably have been making her debut in Newark society. Jeannette, ever anxious to establish an appropriate setting for her only daughter, might have wanted the main rooms redecorated to be up-to-date. The fact that a second doorway was added to the billiard room from the parlor is also telling. Billiards, once the province of men only, had become appropriate not only for women but

THE PARLOR, 1885

THE LIBRARY, 1885

for young women. Making the billiard room part of the entertaining suite suggests that Jeannette would have used these public rooms to present Alice to eligible young men. Finding a good husband for daughters was a serious job for women like Mrs. Ballantine, and such important work demanded the right surroundings. The bills from the firm that took on this redecoration project, Roux & Co., also of New York, have survived as well.

DECORATING BILL

FROM ROUX & CO., 1891

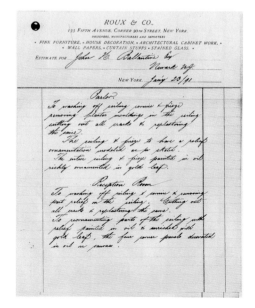

A Tour of
The Ballantine House

The Orientation Gallery

Today you enter the Ballantine House from the north wing of the Museum complex. In fact, the modern glass doors are located where the cooking range originally stood in the kitchen chimney. The entire kitchen was gutted in the 1920s, and only the swinging door into the garden vestibule survives. Even the windows were all replaced. A dumbwaiter, once thought to be original to the house, was discovered to have been built in the 1920s for the insurance company and was removed. The one surviving kitchen door was carefully preserved, but the 1920s windows were all bricked in, and an entirely new gallery, the Orientation Gallery, was designed by the Museum's architect, Michael Graves. The Orientation Gallery provides exhibition space for the Museum's enormous decorative arts collections, ranging from the 1650s to the present, as well as a context for the Ballantine House itself. All decorative arts objects were initially intended for use in people's homes, and the Ballantine House has become a "case study" of how one family used objects to turn its house into a home, according to the precepts of Victorian America.

The Garden Vestibule

This tiny space was the back entrance to the house from the garden, and is now your entrance into the restored house. The family would have used this as its only access to the garden; but the servants would also have used it to get from the kitchen's double-hinged swinging door to the butler's pantry door. You are directly beneath the main staircase landing here.

THE CHILDREN OF

ROBERT F. BALLANTINE,

DETAIL, *above*

THE ENTRANCE HALL

The Entrance Hall

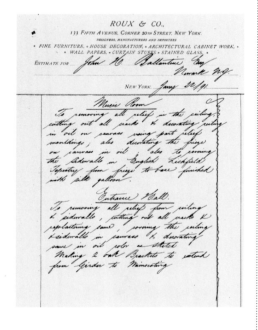

DECORATING BILL FROM ROUX & CO., 1891

The long entrance hall created the visitor's first impression of the house in 1885. It was entirely wainscoted with "calico pattern" oak that continued up the stairway and throughout the second-floor hall. The massive oak mantelpiece is in a late Victorian rendition of the Renaissance style, borrowed loosely from sixteenth-century Italian sources. Mr. Harney would have designed this mantel for the family, and the initial "B" is found on an oval cabochon at the center below the mantel shelf. While confined here in the relatively narrow space of a city house hallway, fireplaces like this were also used in the "living halls" popular for country houses of this period in America; but such fireplaces also evoked images of baronial mansions of Europe, with their associations of power and ancient families.

The great staircase rises from the 14-foot-wide back half of the hall to the second floor, its square newel posts carved in Renaissance-style relief, while the balusters are turned in an elaborate design, possibly suggesting the elaborately turned stair balusters of Colonial Rhode Island. The walls in the entire hallway were originally decorated as those in the staircase part of the hall are today. Paint research revealed that the pattern of repeating shell or fan motifs, "elegantly modeled in a raised relief design artistically worked and colored," was painted with a rich chocolate brown, and then glazed with bronze powder to produce a golden, shimmering effect against the dark ground. The contrast between the dark plaster and the honey color of the woodwork would have been even more pronounced in 1885.

In 1891, this treatment was removed from the 10-foot-wide front part of the front hall and replaced with canvas, painted with Renaissance designs in muted colors. The ceiling here was clearly meant to resemble a coved plasterwork ceiling, while the walls were perhaps meant to look like tooled leather. A polished parquet floor of oak tiles extended the full length of the hallway to the front door, which combined colorful

Aesthetic-style stained glass with an oak overdoor designed to imitate a Colonial mantelpiece from New Jersey.

The stained-glass fanlight over the vestibule doors shows a rising sun, and indeed the red jewels in this glass panel catch the morning sun every day and scatter points of ruby light across the carpeting. The original mottled rusty color has been restored to the ceiling of the staircase hall.

The only original piece of furniture from the hallway is the oak banquette or bench, which today stands where it would have in 1885. It was initially upholstered in painted Portuguese leather, and would have been used as a place to rest while putting on boots, or as a place where visitors who were not considered important could wait. However, both the Moorish-style brass lighting fixtures are original to the hallway. The Renaissance-style marble and bronze mantel clock is original to the house as well. It was probably purchased by the Ballantines for their earlier house, since in 1885 its matching candelabra were used in the reception room.

The fumed oak grandfather clock by the dining room doorway came from the Scudder family home on Washington Place. The works were made by J. & J. Elliott of London, but the case is American. It combines elaborate Colonial Revival and Renaissance details in a way perfectly suited to this hallway. The long buffet and the small carved chest flanking the music room doorway would have been "antiques" for the Ballantines. The buffet is actually the bottom half of an English china hutch of the 1600s, while the carved chest is made up of authentic pieces of Italian carving from the 1500s. The Ballantines and their peers would have appreciated the atmosphere that "antiques" such as these gave to their hall. The rest of the furnishings in the hall are from the Museum collection and represent objects appropriate to the time. The large portrait on the wall is by Benjamin Constant and depicts Robert F. Ballantine, John's younger brother, who lived next door.

The Billiard Room

"WHY NOT ACCEPT THE PASTIME AS ONE OF THE SOCIAL AMUSEMENTS, AND GIVE IT THE SAME PROMINENCE AS MUSIC OR CARDS, AND LET THE BILLIARD-ROOM BE SITUATED ON THE PARLOR STORY, OPENING, IF YOU PLEASE, DIRECTLY INTO THE SITTING-ROOM, WHERE THE LADIES MAY FEEL FREE TO ENTER AND JOIN IN THE GAME IF SO DISPOSED."
—Modern Dwellings, 1878

To the left of the hall fireplace is the single, small doorway into the billiard room. The room was the plainest of all the main-floor rooms, and was wainscoted and trimmed in ash. The beams, however, are oak. It seems that the scheme laid out by Hess in the 1885 estimate was simplified further, probably to cut costs as the project evolved. Because the room was intended only for men to play pocket billiards in, it didn't need to be as elegant or as pretentious as the other rooms. The ash mantelpiece.is the only one in the house with glass-doored cupboards, but it was nonetheless the least expensive one on the floor. The doorway to the right of the fireplace was added in 1891, to tie the room into the parlor and reception room.

In the 1920s, the long wall with the lavatory doorway was removed by the insurance company, and the room was combined with the former kitchen. Because the kitchen wing was lower, the original ceiling beams were left untouched. The ash paneling from that wall was reused to make wainscoting around the new larger room, and the lavatory doorcases were used to make two window frames for the larger space. A fire exit was cut into the wall to the left of the mantelpiece. Over the years, this room had been painted many times, but the mantelpiece was never touched, and provided the correct color for the restoration of the rest of the woodwork. When the west wall was rebuilt, the paneling was restored and put back in place. The deep butterscotch color on the walls replicates the original. The oak flooring survived intact under 1920s linoleum and has been restored. The stained-glass windows in this room were removed, conserved, and put back in place. Their original cost was $105. The elaborate gasolier came from the dining room of the Symington House, which still stands on Military Park in Newark. Given by the Symington family to the Episcopal Diocese of Newark in 1965, the house presently functions as St. Philip's Academy.

DETAIL OF THE BILLIARD TABLE, *above;*

THE BILLIARD ROOM. LEFT

The furnishings in the room are from the Museum's collection, and are appropriate to the period of the house. Of special note is the mahogany pocket-billiard table, by Brunswick, Balke, Collender of Chicago. Made circa 1900, it came from an estate in South Orange, New Jersey. Although the Ballantines' billiard table was probably of a

=ESTIMATE.* New York, _____ 188_

D. S. HESS & CO.,

Warerooms, 376 & 378 Broadway, bet. 18th & 19th Streets,
Factory, 145, 147, 149 & 151 Eleventh Avenue, cor. 21st Street.

Artistic Furniture, Interior Wood-work & Decorations.

For _____

		Forward	$782 —
Billiard Room	Ceiling frescoed in an appropriate design shown		
	Walls painted with 5 coats of best English Oil paint in color selected	118 —	
	Frieze painted in style shown—		
	Picture mouldings to match		
Drawing Room	Ceiling decorated in a highly artistic manner, after special Drawing submitted - Colors to be light and elegant in harmony with hangings A frieze to be elegantly hand painted on canvas		
	Sidewalls to be suitably lined and prepared and draped in Crème Lampas, specially made in full width Picture mouldings to match	980 —	
Reception Room	Ceiling richly arranged in a combination of tastefully metallized Beadings and motives to harmonize with Satin Damask on Walls		
	Sidewalls prepared all the way up to Cove and hung in finest silk Damask as selected and furnished over entire wall without frieze at top	854 —	
	Forward	$2734 —	

lighter wood than this, the simple style is in keeping with the overall plainness of the room. The Aesthetic-style mahogany chairs, with their original black leather seats, came from the Symington House in Newark. They are dining chairs, and were the kind of chair typically used in billiard rooms in this period. The exotic little marble-topped table has a

NEEDLEWORK PICTURE
BY MARY D. HAGEMAN,
1882-1889, *opposite page;*
DECORATING INVOICE FOR
THE BILLIARD ROOM, 1885, *left*

base made of steer horns. Such furniture was made in Texas and Chicago as well as New York and is peculiar to America in the 1880s. Horn parlor tables are especially rare, and this one was purchased by the Museum specifically for use in this room, to accompany the stuffed animal heads used as decoration. The presence of animal heads does not imply that Mr. Ballantine was a hunter, however. Decorators provided these as they would any decorative accessory for fashionable interiors. The patent mechanical spittoon, disguised by its stylish walnut case, is a rare survival of the 1870s. One can imagine Jeannette Ballantine insisting that it be used rather than an open spittoon. A lady's influence can also be seen in the massive needlework picture between the sconces on the west wall. Worked by Mary D. Hageman of Princeton between 1882 and 1889, it depicts Mary Queen of Scots being turned over to the forces of her nemesis, Queen Elizabeth I. Such an image would have been right at home with a family of Scottish descent such as the Ballantines.

NEEDLEWORK PICTURE

BY MARY D. HAGEMAN,

1882-1889

The Parlor

This was Jeannette Ballantine's room. Here she demonstrated herself to be both a leader in society and a follower of the best taste of her day. It was a very modern room in 1885. It was an "evening" room—the wide bay window always faced north into another building, so good daylight was not a necessary feature. This room was all about being inside, about gaslight glittering on gold and jewels and silks. The wainscoting and woodwork in this room were of the only soft wood in the house—pine—because it was always covered in several coats of ivory paint and then richly ornamented in gold leaf. The tone of the room was seen as "French," in the eclectic eyes of the 1880s, but the doorcases and mantelpiece were in the modern Colonial Revival style. According to specifications, the mantelpiece, with a polished onyx interior surround, cost $250. The silvered brass firebox surround, with its matching fender and andirons, were all Renaissance in style, as are the original silvered sconces. Even the remarkable English figural fireplace tiles, with a rich pink ground predominating, are derived from sixteenth-century Italian sources, reinterpreted for the nineteenth century. Originally, the room had an elaborate Aesthetic-style ceiling, with plaster

DETAIL OF THE PARLOR, *above*

DETAIL OF FIREPLACE TILES,

PARLOR, *above*

THE PARLOR, LEFT

DETAIL OF PARLOR SCONCE

strapwork and gold stenciled designs in the Japanese taste. But in 1891 Roux & Co. came in to make the room even more modern. An additional Colonial Revival doorway was added to the left of the fireplace, connecting the room with the billiard room, thus enlarging the entertainment suite by thirty percent. The Japanesque ceiling was replaced with one based on designs by the eighteenth-century English architect Robert Adam. Adam's work was very famous in England and America in the 1880s, and it blended well with Colonial Revival fashions. It was also, not coincidentally, sympathetic to French taste of the eighteenth century. Thus it was an ideal way to tie the room together into something less eclectic in 1891. The 1885 frieze was replaced with one of low-relief plaster wreaths, and then it and the ceiling were enriched with gold leaf to coordinate with the woodwork. The walls were covered with an ivory damask, which was replaced with an appropriate facsimile in 1976.

During the period when the house was used for business offices, two small windows were added to the short walls at either end of the parlor's bay window. These were removed in the 1976 restoration, and the lost sections of the plaster frieze were restored. The intricate plaster ceiling had survived but was much weakened and needed to be cleaned, painted, and regilded. Because the plaster ornament was applied first to canvas that had been glued to the plaster to create a smooth surface, it was necessary to secure the canvas to the ceiling before any surface conservation could begin. Glue was injected behind the canvas to adhere it to the plaster ceiling.

The ceiling was regilded, as were the mantelpiece, wainscoting, and doorcases. These all had also been overpainted many times. For the 1994 restoration, the ceiling needed additional conservation work, due to the lack of climate control.

The silver-gilt gas sconces, which had survived in place, were cleaned and wired for electricity. The crystal and brass electric chandelier, from the Robert Ballantine House next door, was also restored for the 1994 project. The white pine floor was sanded in 1976 and stained to resemble a dark hardwood, its original finish. Dark-stained, inexpensive pine was apparently used because the room was always intended to have a large Persian carpet, which covered most of the floor area. The 1885 bay window draperies survived, but the fabric had deteriorated beyond repair. Silk and velvet that matched the original in color and texture were selected for the new draperies in 1976. The original velvet and gilt appliqués were cut by hand from the old draperies and sewn on to the new ones. Elaborate silk tiebacks, fringes, and tassels were copied from the existing originals.

DETAIL OF MICRO-MOSAIC TABLETOP

MICRO-MOSAIC TABLETOP, CIRCA 1891

HERTS BROTHERS CABINET, PARLOR

The clutter of the parlor was quite intentional. Beauty was the only useful attribute of a parlor, and its function as a room was to dazzle. Variety of form, texture, and color was considered vital to such rooms in the late Victorian era. Rooms were meant to be richly layered and to be enjoyed at leisure—not unlike the long novels of the period. Everything was meant to coordinate, but nothing needed to match. The elaborate enameled ormolu clock and candelabra on the mantelpiece—complete with their original gilt-trimmed wax candles!—were on the mantelpiece in 1885. The English porcelains and French ivory figurines are all similar to those that would have been there originally. A significant suite of American-made furniture original to the room survives. It is much faded from its original lushness, but gives a clear indication of the effect the room was supposed to give in 1891. The Napoleonic-style armchair near the reception room doorway is trimmed in orange silk plush, and originally the silk needlework panels would have been brilliant and lustrous—shimmering in the flickering of the gas sconces. The two little mahogany chairs by the tea table—both French in style, but quite different from each other—were trimmed in different colored silk plushes, with coordinated silk cording and different patterned silk needlepoint seatcovers. The little gilt bamboo-turned footstool near the fireplace also was trimmed in electric blue silk plush, with a silk petit-point floral design on top. Mrs. Ballantine might have worked some of these seat covers herself, to show off her talents. All these have faded to mere ghosts of their former selves, but nevertheless remain extremely rare and important documents of late Victorian upholstery.

The gilt center table, with its splendid micro-mosaic tabletop, is original to the house. These mosaic tabletops were made of tiny bits of glass in Italian workshops (both in Rome and in Florence). Wealthy American tourists purchased them as souvenirs of their travels. Scenes of the famous tourist attractions of Rome, in minute detail, are bordered in malachite and set into a black slate frame. On this table sits an elaborate porcelain and ormolu kerosene lamp in the Japanese style. The Ballantines would always have used oil lamps in addition to their gas fixtures, as the 1885 photographs indicate. The fine gilt mounts on this lamp were made in New York City, by Peter E. Guerin & Company, but the hand-painted porcelain body of the lamp was imported.

Near the center table, by the billiard room doorway, is the mahogany vitrine cabinet (*vitre* being the French word for window glass—vitrines were glass-fronted display cupboards) with its gilt mounts and inset onyx top. This splendid object, with shelves of glass or lined in silk velvet, was intended only to hold more elegant and costly knickknacks, and was made by Herts Brothers in New York City. Most likely made for the redecoration in 1891, it combines several French and English motifs in a suitably eclectic way.

The fine marble-topped corner cupboards and tea table are in fact French made, and came from a New York City townhouse. They were made in the 1870s or 1880s and are typical of the imported French reproduction furniture used in American homes. The smaller vitrine cabinet in the corner by the reception room belonged to Alice Ballantine Young.

PARLOR LAMP, CIRCA 1880

The Reception Room

The reception room, to the right of the front entry, had wainscoting and woodwork in carefully matched figured maple. Its light, blond tone was meant to contrast strongly with the dark woodwork of the "family" rooms across the hall, and to blend with the ivory and gold of the parlor beyond. Time has probably darkened the woodwork to the familiar honey tone we see now. The carved mantelpiece, with its carefully worked out Renaissance-style details, cost $150. The walls were initially covered in a green silk damask and the ceiling was ornamented with painted and relief-molded plaster, as shown in the 1885 photograph of the room. The floor had ash and cherry perimeter bands with a large pine center section. As in the parlor, the floor was meant to be largely hidden by an oriental rug, and thus it was seen as wasteful to install hardwoods in areas that would be covered. In 1891, as part of the alterations to the entertainment rooms, the relief-molded ceiling was "washed off and replastered," according to the redecorating estimates. Roux & Co. specified changes such as "reornamenting parts of the ceiling with relief painted in oil and enriched with gold leaf, the four corner panels decorated in oil on canvas." The cornices were repainted with tones of olive and brown, highlighted with gold, and an ultra-modern imitation leather paper from Germany was put up. Its textured brown surface and embossed gold Art Nouveau border would have been extremely avant-garde for the time. This room had survived relatively intact, and in 1976 only cleaning and restoration of the ceiling painting, as well as regilding of the plaster relief, was needed. Draperies

DETAIL OF SECRETARY

and fringes were copied from those visible in the 1885 photograph of the room and Victorian sconces replaced twentieth-century fixtures. In the reception room, as well as throughout the house, the original hardwood interior shutters were numbered, removed for conservation, cleaned, and finally reinstalled.

The andirons and the gray marble candelabra on the mantelpiece survive from the original fittings of the room. The red and white cameo glass vase on the mantelpiece is placed where it was in 1885. The bronze firebox frame and the iron firebox itself, as well as the Middle Eastern-style J. & J.G. Low art tiles, survived intact. The three-piece parlor suite in brown velveteen is from the 1860s, and represents the sort of furniture the Ballantines would have recovered for use in the new house. The Elizabethan-style reception chair with its yellow silk seat dates from the 1850s. It was made for Newark Mayor Moses Bigelow by Jelliff & Co., but is identical to one owned by the Ballantine family and used in this room in 1885. The other reception chair in this style also is identical to one used here in 1885. Again by Jelliff & Co., it was originally in the Van Antwerp House at 53 Washington Street, built in 1858.

The gilt center table is Italian and has a top of inlaid hardstone (known as *pietra dura*). It was purchased by a Newark family at the Philadelphia Centennial Exposition in 1876 and is similar to the table used here in 1885. The large secretary desk in maple is the sort of piece John and Jeannette Ballantine might have purchased in the 1880s as an "antique." The piece is actually from the third quarter of the eighteenth century, but new carving was added to it, and new finials and feet were made in the 1880s.

Such additions were typical of the way antique furniture was "improved" by furniture makers and antique dealers in this period. Customers like the Ballantines might easily have requested such improvements—and been willing to pay extra for them. Antiques were not expensive in the 1880s, but they were fashionable and added an aura of Colonial respectability to any home. The gasolier is from the 1880s, and came from the Symington House on Park Place.

The Front Vestibule

This little room has its original English encaustic tiled floor and its original woodwork. It is covered floor to ceiling with oak paneling, heavily varnished, to protect it from dampness. The massive oak outer doors also protect the inner doors, with their stained-glass panels and fanlight. The outer semicircular transom bears the large gilt number 43, the last residential address on Washington Park. The stained-glass fanlight faces east and represents the rising sun. An umbrella stand and a bench for sitting on while removing one's boots would have been the only furnishings.

JELLIFF ROSEWOOD
RECEPTION CHAIR, 1850s

A FRONT DOOR WINDOW

THE RECEPTION ROOM

The Library

"IN EVERY HOUSE WHERE IT IS PRACTICABLE THERE SHOULD BE A ROOM SPECIALLY DEVOTED TO QUIET AND RETIREMENT...FOR THE PURPOSES OF STUDY, WRITING OR READING." — Beautiful Homes, 1878

"THE ROOM SHOULD BE SURROUNDED WITH BOOKCASES, THE LOWER PORTION... COVERED IN WITH CUPBOARD FRONTS...THE SHELF WHICH THIS LOWER PROJECTION FORMS WILL DO ADMIRABLY FOR THE ARRANGEMENT OF ORNAMENTS, SMALL BUSTS, OR OTHER PERSONAL THINGS." — Decoration of Furniture of Town Houses, 1881

The library was really the family room of the house. If any room on this floor allowed for casual behavior and comfort for the entire family, this was it. The darkness of the room would have been relieved by the wide expanses of glass and sunlight all day long. The wainscoting, doorcases, and the spectacular mantelpiece and overmantel are all of cherry. In order to save a little money, the shelves and backs of the bookcases were made of pine with a cherry stain. The elaborate carved floor-to-ceiling mantelpiece and overmantel cost $250 and combine accurate renderings of Renaissance detail with thoroughly modern touches, such as the Colonial Revival arcade of carved fans and the little carved rosettes or "pies," which were inspired by Japanese motifs. The bronze firebox surround, iron firebox, and American art tiles all survive untouched. The ceiling and walls of the room were also inspired by Japanese and Persian ideas, and have remained as they were in 1885—a particularly rare survival of the period. The decorator called for the plasterwork to be

> modeled and colored in a highly artistic manner appropriate to the shape and style of the room, the tone of room to be a soft Old Red, the frieze, a hanging fringe as shown, with a fine low relief design below in Conventional pattern over the Wainscoting, there is to be modeled a suitable border in keeping with the Wall, the entire color tone of Ceiling and Walls to be a quiet harmony of blended Old Red and old Metals.

The estimated cost for the library decoration, exclusive of the woodwork, was $422. During its office years, the plasterwork was painted various colors, but during the 1976

DETAIL OF
MR BALLANTINE'S DESK

restoration a modern wall sconce was removed and the original "Old Red" color was revealed. The raised plaster relief designs and the "fringed" plaster frieze were gilded with gold leaf. For the ceiling, Dutch metal leaf, a combination of brass and gold, was applied. Slightly less lustrous than gold leaf, it must be coated to prevent tarnishing. The plaster beams were also repaired and painted.

The subject of the stained-glass window in the library was based on John Ballantine's original suggestion; the design and manufacture is attributed to Tiffany Studios. Painter Elihu Vedder worked for Louis C. Tiffany during this period, and the window evokes his painterly style. A strikingly modern Art Nouveau composition for 1885, the window is an allegory of the family name, derived from the Scottish Gaelic words *bael*, meaning fire, and *antin*, a worshiper. The window depicts a Celtic maiden worshiping the sun, as smoke from an incense burner rises skyward. According to family tradition, John Ballantine was disappointed with the finished window, feeling that the colors were dull and did not suggest the light and fire as he had intended. Certainly it is not as vibrant and colorful as the hall windows, but it is far more sophisticated artistically. Hess ordered all the windows for the Ballantine House, for which the estimate survives. The figure window in the library, at $460, cost more than the decoration for the entire room, and three times as much per square foot as the other windows in the house, further supporting the attribution to an especially fine maker.

The only original furnishings in the room are John Ballantine's easy chair and his desk. The mahogany easy chair is a rare Victorian version of the Morris armchair, popularized by the celebrated English social reformer and designer, William Morris. The back is adjustable, using a brass rod. The chair retains its original cut silk velvet upholstery, which was blue, but has oxidized over the years to a dark olive. Another, simpler mahogany Morris chair with red leather upholstery continues the effect of comfort in the room. The Renaissance-style cherry fall-front desk may have been designed by Harney himself; in any case it was certainly designed for the room. Its back rail is cut out to make it fit precisely in the corner where it sits. This is a working desk, full of drawers and pigeon holes, and with locks to secure important papers. The desk's interior finish, undarkened by time, shows the original color of the woodwork of the entire room.

INVOICE FOR

STAINED-GLASS WINDOWS

FROM D.S. HESS & CO., 1885

The bronze busts on the mantelpiece, representing Albrecht Dürer, the sixteenth-century German Renaissance artist, and Rembrandt, were originally in this house, and were produced by French artist Ernest Carrier-Belleuse. Stores such as Tiffany & Co. specialized in this sort of *objet d'art*. A third reclining chair, to the left of the doorway, was patented in Brooklyn by George Hunzinger & Co. in the 1860s. It retains its original silk plush and needlework upholstery. The arms have a series of notches, like present-day lawn furniture, to allow the back to adjust.

The bronze gasolier is similar to the one that originally hung here. The wheels visible at the top demonstrate that it was adjustable, as library gasoliers often were, to allow it to be pulled lower, toward the center table, for reading. The red velvet drapery arrangement approximates the 1885 design and utilizes a gold thread fringe manufactured in 1890.

THE LIBRARY, *previous spread;*

MR. BALLANTINE'S DESK

The Music Room

Behind the library was the music room, also featuring cherry woodwork. The only architectural features of note in this room are the doorcases, of a broadly Colonial Revival style, each one with a masterful little Rococo carved panel in the center. Hardly more than a passageway between library and dining room, the music room was, however, lavishly decorated and furnished as a sitting room. When the parlor and reception room were not being used for parties, the music room would have added a useful space to the family suite on this side of the first floor. The ceiling, according to the Hess estimates, was originally decorated in "Old Blue" with "Chaste illumination in quiet harmony with [the] wall." The side walls were hung with imported blue silk moiré. The cost of the decoration was $360—a great deal for a small room. In 1891, the plaster ceiling decorations were removed and canvas was placed over the ceiling. The Roux & Co. estimate specified "decorating ceiling in oil on canvas using part relief mouldings." The blue moiré fabric ordered in 1885 was removed and English tapestry was installed in its place. A beadwork firescreen worked by Jeannette Ballantine was originally in this room—an oddity in a music room with no fireplace (and no piano). That firescreen was probably used for the library fireplace when needed, and is presently displayed in the master bedroom.

MUSIC ROOM CEILING

BEING RESTORED, 1976

The furnishings in this room are either reproductions or pieces used for educational purposes. In 1976, this room was restored as a gallery, with exhibition cases for small objects. Although a useful place for exhibitions, it was decided that the house needed a room where visitors could "get the feel" of what it was like to live in a house like this. One of the library's Morris chairs has been recreated in a simpler version by New Jersey cabinetmaker Dean Squires, along with a footstool, to allow visitors to sit down and put their feet up. A Colonial Revival desk, as well as a dressing mirror and vitrine cabinet, are placed here to encourage exploration and discovery. The sconces are reproductions and replace modern fixtures added during the 1930s.

Parquet flooring in the hall, library, and music room presented special problems. Years of heavy use had worn these floors down to 1/4 inch in thickness, and replacement was the only answer. In 1976, specially milled oak parquet squares in block and herringbone designs were installed in all three rooms. The original cherry, ash, and oak borders were left in place.

The Dining Room

Used both by the family every day and to impress guests at dinner parties, the dining room was as large and grand as the parlor, but designed to endure more use. It was clearly John Ballantine's room, where he presided as the breadwinner over his board and family. It was meant to be dark and rich, and to evoke baronial palaces. The lavish use of mahogany was carried throughout the room; from the wainscoting, with its lushly carved Renaissance panel over the serving table; to the great mantelpiece and overmantel, with its carved panels flanking the portrait; to the ceiling with its massive (and purely decorative) beams. This was the third $250 carved mantelpiece on the first floor. As in all the first-floor rooms, the dining room has massive sliding pocket doors faced with the same wood as the woodwork in the room. The ceiling was composed of cast and gilt papier-mâché relief-molded panels that were ornamented with foliate and fruit designs illuminated in what the decorator called "Antique Metal." The walls, miraculously, retain their "heavily raised Antique Leather Paper with edges top and bottom finished with Leather galloons and large Antique Nails." This high-tech wallpaper cost $390 in 1885—more than the decoration of the music room.

The pattern of convoluted floral and fruit designs of the dining room paper is identical to a design manufactured in Yokohama and Tokyo, Japan, by the London firm of Rottman Strome & Co. The company had American salesrooms at 19 East 21st Street, New York, just a few blocks from the D.S. Hess warerooms. The paper was illustrated in the July 1885 issue of American Decorator and Furnisher, published in New York. In advertising the wallpaper, Rottman Strome & Co. claimed:

> *Our Japanese Leathers are now largely used in connection with the Queen Anne style and the Flemish Renaissance, and admired for their harmony in colour and superior finish.... The new Papers for Diningrooms, Libraries, Clubs, Theatres, Halls, Staircases, & C. will stand moist walls, and can be cleaned with soap and water.*

The Ballantine paper was a competing brand of a famous product called Lincrusta-Walton Japanese leather paper. The technique was invented by an Englishman, Frederick Walton,

MAHOGANY PANEL. 1885

in 1877. After first experimenting with linoleum applied to wall surfaces, Walton developed a new material composed primarily of solidified linseed oil that he embossed in elaborate designs. He called it *Lincrusta*—*lin* for the Latin *linium* (flax) and *crusta* for relief. The new product was unequaled in its flexibility and resilience. The fact that it has survived a century in downtown Newark is testimony to its durability.

Dutch metal leaf was also used to highlight fruit and foliate motifs on the dining room wallpaper. The papier-mâché ceiling panels were regilded to complement the wall. Certain areas of the chevron parquet flooring were replaced, but eighty percent of the original flooring was saved.

Two stained-glass windows in the dining room (which cost $163 in 1885) feature Japanesque designs in shades of blue, ocher and rust, and green, with grapes and vines

THE DINING ROOM

draping across stylized trellises. The food imagery in the wallpaper, ceiling panels, carved woodwork, and the windows all refer to the opulence and plenty of the Ballantines' dinners, and are an outward show of Victorian hospitality. Such imagery was on the wane in the 1880s, and this room is a remarkably rich surviving example of it. The light coming through these southern exposure windows was so brilliant that Mr. and Mrs. Ballantine, who formerly sat at the north and south ends of the table, changed the orientation of the table to east-west.

The mahogany dining chairs, which retain their original "bronze" tapestry, were part of a set of ten. They, like the walnut sideboard, are in the Renaissance style, but the sideboard came from the Symington House on Military Park. It was produced by Kirk & Jacobus, the same firm that did the woodwork in the room. The elaborate stained walnut china cupboard belonged to Alice Ballantine Young and was used in her third-floor living room/library. While the 1885 decorator's specifications listed brass drapery equipment in the library and reception room, for the dining room copper rods and fixtures were ordered, from which hang reproduction tapestry curtains. Likewise, the flamboyant copper gasolier reflects the original decorator's specification, although this one was purchased in 1976.

Behind the dining room was an ash paneled butler's pantry that extended across to the kitchen, where there were stairs leading both to the cellar and to the servants' quarters on the second floor.

THE STAIR LANDING

FROM THE SECOND FLOOR,

following page

DETAIL OF

MAGOGANY PANEL, 1885

The Stair Landing

"THE STAIRCASE SHOULD BE WELL SET IN THE HALL, NOT TOO NEAR THE DOOR, VERY BROAD, WITH A SOLID BALUSTRADE AND HAND-RAIL, THE UPPER HALL WITH ITS OWN BALUSTRADE SUSPENDED IN SUCH A WAY AS TO OBTAIN FOR IT A LIGHT GALLERY-LIKE LOOK. LOW WIDE STEPS SHOULD MAKE THE FLIGHT, ALL THE BETTER IF BROKEN INTO LANDINGS."

—Art Decoration Applied to Furniture, 1877

The staircase was initially designed to be 6 feet wide by Harney, but it was narrowed to 5 feet, according to the original plans. The focal point of the stairs is the great stained-glass window at the landing, ordered through D.S. Hess & Co. in 1885 at a cost of about $592 (the front doors and fanlight probably cost $176). Made up of twelve panels, the window is in the Japanesque manner popularized during the Aesthetic Movement. It faces due west, and evokes the setting sun over a garden of exotic jeweled flowers. With its crackle pattern and bright turquoise glass (which changes to lavender in strong sunlight), it seems to evoke cloisonné enamels, and is surprisingly abstract and modern. Such large windows were typical for landings in city houses in the 1880s, and they were in part intended to provide light while obscuring unromantic urban scenery. Although the Ballantines had a large garden lined with fruit trees, there were also small working-class rowhouses and factories within sight of the house. This glamorous, colorful window successfully hid all this from view.

Flanking the original oak banquette, upon which family members might have paused to read a letter, or a servant might have paused to catch her breath, are a pair of monumental porcelain urns, painted with scenes from Wagner's opera *Lohengrin*. Made in Berlin or Vienna, these urns came from the Symington House on Military Park in Newark. Facing each other from opposite walls of the landing are the full-length portraits of John and Jeannette Ballantine, painted in 1890 by French artist Benjamin Constant, at a cost of $4000 each. The massive gilt frames (which were about $95 each) once again stand out from the dark shimmering surface of the walls, as they were meant to do in 1890. One can imagine John and Jeannette coming down to breakfast each day and pausing to admire their portraits, a reminder of who they were in Newark and what they had accomplished in their lives.

BENJAMIN CONSTANT, PORTRAITS OF

JOHN AND JEANNETTE BALLANTINE, 1890

The Second-Floor Hall

All the family passed through this hallway. Only the servants could have moved, unseen, from the kitchen to their rooms above. The entire second floor was carpeted wall to wall in 1885, and it has been similarly treated during the restoration. The painted finishes here reflect the 1885 treatments, which do not appear to have been altered during the family's occupancy. The bronzed shell-pattern plasterwork from the first floor continues to the second-floor archway, beyond which a simpler glazed surface was used. The original color scheme on the cornice and walls was recreated based on paint analysis.

Former Servants' Wing

In the largest of these spaces were originally three of the maids' rooms designed by Harney. The two smaller spaces had been allocated to Percy Ballantine's dressing room and the fourth maid's room as well as a walk-in linen closet. All these partitions had been entirely removed by the insurance company in the 1920s, and two large skylights had been inserted in the ceiling. Only two of the original servants' wing windows survived. These have been carefully preserved, and are still visible from the exterior of the house.

The galleries in the former servants' wing are used to display the Museum's decorative arts collections, as well as for the interactive computer game and the video gallery.

PERCY BALLANTINE'S

BEDROOM MANTEL

Percy Ballantine's Former Bedroom

This space, one of the three gallery rooms on this floor, originally encompassed Percy Ballantine's bedroom, the bathroom he shared with his parents, and his parents' dressing closets. A short passageway led from Percy's room to the sliding pocket door of the master bedroom.

The original ash woodwork survives intact, but the color scheme on the walls and cornice has been left neutral, using an appropriate nineteenth-century hue. The 1885 Colonial Revival mantelpiece, fireplace fittings, shutters, and heating grill have been left in place. New track lighting was installed in 1994. The room is used for exhibiting decorative arts objects from the collection, ranging from the 1650s to the present day.

The Master Bedroom

"MANY PEOPLE NOW-A-DAYS PREFER, ON SANITARY GROUNDS, TO SLEEP…IN BEDS WITHOUT HANGINGS OF ANY KIND."   —Hints on Household Taste, 1878

"CARPETS ARE NOW SO UNIVERSALLY USED TO COVER EVERY PORTION OF THE FLOORS… THAT FEW PEOPLE FIND THEMSELVES COMFORTABLE WITHOUT ONE."
      —Hints on Household Taste, 1878

This was the largest bedroom in the house, and although on the north corner, it looked out over Washington Park, which remains much as it was a century ago. John and Jeannette Ballantine shared a bedroom throughout their married life. Even in their new house, which had eight bedrooms and three sitting rooms on two floors, they kept only one bedroom for themselves. In the late Victorian era, this was fairly uncommon for people of their wealth; in fact, separate bedrooms were seen by many people as healthier for married couples. A room like this reminds us that the ideal Victorian marriage was based on affection and mutual companionship.

Only the hallway on the second floor had wainscoting. The master bedroom has cherry woodwork and exotic mottled blue tiles, most likely English, around the fireplace opening. All the bedrooms relied on colorful cornice moldings and modern wallpapers for their decoration. Only Percy's bedroom was originally painted rather than papered.

The 1885 decorating bills that survive for the second floor, indicate that some of the decoration might have been eliminated to cut costs, but the painted cornices and papered walls were carried out as specified.

For the 1994 restoration, a special hand-printed wallpaper was chosen, reproducing an English Aesthetic design called "Bachelor's Buttons". The soft, smoky blue-green color was selected as a complement to the woodwork and the claret red wool carpeting. The carpeting was produced in Belgium by the same company that had designed it in the nineteenth century. Jacquard looms wove the 27-inch-wide strips, which were sewn together on site and installed with brass nails, as they would have been in 1885. In both the master bedroom and the boudoir, designs from the 1870s have been selected in order to reflect the middle-aged John and Jeannette's slightly more conservative taste.

The gasolier in the master bedroom came from the Symington House on Military Park. Although rewired in the 1920s by the Symington family, and again for this restoration, the fixture retains its original lacquered finish. The mahogany bed and chest of drawers (called a dressing bureau) are in a style that would have been called Anglo-Japanese in 1885. They came from a New Jersey family, which had purchased them in 1889 for their home in Spring Lake. The circular mirror on the dresser is meant to recall

SECOND-FLOOR

DECORATING INVOICE, 1885

a Japanese "moon gate," and the stylized low-relief carvings are also meant to appear Japanese. However, the relief sculpture on the headboard of the bed would have been immediately recognized by any cultured Victorian; it is based on the celebrated sculpture *Dawn*, by Danish artist Bertel Thorvaldsen (1770-1844). The same design, in beadwork, is seen on the mahogany-framed firescreen, worked by Mrs. Ballantine and used originally (if oddly) in the music room. This, along with the malachite-inlaid garniture set on the mantelpiece, are the only Ballantine family pieces in the room. The small table, with its ornate marquetry top, is of rosewood, and was produced in Newark by Jelliff & Co. in the 1870s. The little ebonized side chair, with its marquetry panel of Japanese-style flowers, was produced by Herter Brothers in New York City. Similar chairs were installed in the Red Room at the White House in the late 1870s by President Ulysses S. Grant. The silk-upholstered platform rocker is in the Turkish style of the 1880s, and the reproduction lace curtains use a design that was exhibited at the Centennial Exposition in Philadelphia in 1876. It would have been typical in the period for bedrooms not to have heavy draperies, but to rely on wooden shutters and light embroidered muslin or lace curtains.

The Boudoir

*"THE BOUDOIR IS USUALLY AN UP-STAIRS ROOM, ADJOINING THE BEDCHAMBER…AND
NOT TOO FAR FROM THE NURSERY…WE WILL FIND IN THE BOUDOIR…ALL ONE'S PRECIOUS
KNICKKNACKS NOT QUITE NICE ENOUGH FOR THE DRAWING-ROOM…AND WE WILL SEE
THAT IT IS A PLACE OF SOFT COLORS, SOFT CARPETS AND CURTAINS…"*

—Art Decoration Applied to Furniture, 1877

The boudoir was the smallest room, other than the maids' rooms, on the second floor. *Bouder* in French means "to pout," and the term was applied to rooms where women could be alone. This small space was in fact the warm heart of the twenty-seven-room Ballantine House. It was the control room of this great social battleship, and from here Mrs. Ballantine kept track of her social and domestic world. It not only served as her dressing room, but was shared with her teenage daughter, with whose bedroom it connects. In this room, Jeannette was linked architecturally with her husband and her only living daughter.

The plain woodwork here is of hazel, a wood more commonly called sweet gum. It was light in color and smooth in grain, but less costly than maple or cherry. The real luxury of the room would have been in its decoration and furnishings. Elaborate reproduction lace curtains screen the bay window, from which all of Washington Park can be surveyed. The cornice was restored to its original multicolored scheme using paint analysis, and an appropriate Victorian wallpaper, called "Rowland," was picked for the walls. Unlike the other rooms on this floor, the ceiling in the boudoir was also papered. A coordinating paper, called "Ice Blossoms," was selected. The dark olive-green carpet, with its repeating pattern in beige, echoes the wall treatment in the hallway. The only family objects in the room are the delicate mahogany Colonial Revival desk chair and the small painting by George Linen of the Robert F. Ballantine children, painted around 1880.

Perhaps Jeannette kept this souvenir of her brother-in-law's children in this private room, rather than on public view downstairs. Other furnishings represent the sort of eclectic mixture of things with which Jeannette would have surrounded herself in her inner sanctum. A sycamore lady's desk, possibly made in Newark, has the script monogram

THE BOUDOIR, *opposite page*

CHILDREN OF ROBERT F. BALLANTINE, *above*

of its original owner on the lid. Lady's desks were distinct forms, and much smaller than men's desks. A lady was supposed to write letters, invitations, and other polite correspondence, while her husband used a large desk for business and other "weighty" matters. However sexist it seems today, it was accepted in 1885. In any case, a delicate little desk like this was ideal for a room like the boudoir. A small Napoleonic-style settee and its matching side chair came from the O'Crowley family of Newark, and the ornately inlaid dressing bureau, by R.J. Horner of New York City, came from the Symington family. There was no ceiling fixture in this room in the nineteenth century, and Jeannette would have relied on a small kerosene lamp, like the one you see here, for light.

Alice Ballantine's Bedroom

"SO FAR AS POSSIBLE ALL THE ROOMS IN THIS IDEAL HOUSE OF OURS FRONT THE SUN, OR ARE VISITED BY THE SUN FOR AN HOUR OR TWO EVERY DAY. I HOLD THIS ALMOST ESSENTIAL TO A BEDROOM." —The House Beautiful, 1877

While not the largest bedroom, Alice's was definitely the sunniest. Not only was it on the south corner of the house, but it had its own bay window and window seat—unique in the house. Sunlight and fresh air were seen as the best deterrents to disease in the era before miracle drugs, which may account for Alice's having this room. The use of hazel (sweet gum) woodwork is repeated in this room, and the finely carved mantelpiece is of the same wood. There is evidence that both Alice's room and her parents' room had open shelves over the mantelpieces, but these have long since disappeared. In their place, a Chinese teakwood display shelf, owned by Alice Ballantine Young and used in the adjacent sewing room, has been placed on the mantel, to hold personal treasures such as might have been collected by a teenage girl in the 1880s.

The gasolier, retaining its original lacquered finish, came from the Symington House in Newark. Reproduction lace curtains hang at the windows, and the dark olive-green carpeting, with its foliate pattern in black, is based on motifs from a Persian carpet. The celadon wallpaper, with its overall pattern of gold branches, is known as "Claire's Willow," and was hand-printed from a nineteenth-century design. The design of the carpet and

wallpaper are the most modern of the three upstairs rooms, as one might expect an adolescent girl to have chosen in 1885.

None of Alice's original bedroom furnishings survive. The bedroom set (or suit as it was called in 1885) is of blonde sycamore and was produced by Jelliff & Co. of Newark. Finely made, it combines Middle Eastern and Renaissance motifs in a typically eclectic Victorian way, although the overall simplicity of the forms shows the influence of aesthetic reformer and tastemaker Charles Locke Eastlake. The marvelous wicker "peacock" chair by the bay window was made in the Philippines, and was used in the Symington House in Newark in the late nineteenth century.

ALICE BALLANTINE'S BEDROOM

Alice's bedroom originally had a small dressing room with a walk-in closet, which connected in turn to the sewing room, or guest sitting room. These spaces were combined into one office in the 1920s, although the shutters and woodwork were carefully preserved. This is the second of the gallery rooms, and has been given a neutral color scheme and modern track lighting, to better display decorative arts objects from the Museum collections. The theme of this gallery is objects that symbolize family relationships.

Former Guest Room

This bedroom is the only one to survive with its built-in closet and bathroom. The bathroom was drastically altered in the 1920s, but the closet has lost only its bronze clothing hooks. According to the 1885 specifications, all the closets had "as much shelving as practicable, an average of three dove-tailed drawers, 18 bronze hooks in each, put where directed by owner." Once again, in this, the third of the gallery rooms, a neutral color scheme and new track lighting have been used, but the original bed niche and fireplace, as well as all the stained birch woodwork have been preserved. The fireplace is a particularly important document: apart from the fine carving, it uses the "Tempus Fugit" design from the J. & J.G. Low Art Tile Works of Chelsea, Massachusetts. It is the only complete fireplace surround in the house that can be documented to a surviving trade catalogue from the 1880s, a replica of which is in the Museum's library. The present theme of this gallery is that of comfort, and how the idea of comfort, as seen through upholstery, lighting, and heating, has developed over time to make the American home a more comfortable and convenient place.

THE GUEST ROOM MANTEL

The Third Floor

The third floor is today used for Museum functions and staff meetings. Except for the little front room over the boudoir, which was originally a sitting room and retains its unpainted ash woodwork, all the 1885 rooms now have white-painted woodwork. This was probably first done in 1900 when Alice Ballantine Young made this floor her family's apartment. By 1900 the dark woodwork of the house would have been seen as inappropriate and unsanitary for children's bedrooms, and shiny white enamel would have replaced the old dark finishes. The green room, made from two bedrooms and their adjoining dressing closets in the 1920s, has been papered with a Victorian reproduction paper called "Persis." All the room's architectural features survive intact.

The yellow room, originally a bedroom, retains its original fitted closet and charming Colonial Revival fireplace with English tiles. It is presently used as a small conference room.

The catering kitchen serves as a warming pantry for dinners in the Trustees' Room. A wheelchair ramp connects this room with the third floor of the Museum's north wing. Despite its modern use, the fireplace, fitted closet, shutters, and even the original wooden doorstops survive from 1885, when it comprised a bedroom and bathroom.

The present Trustees' Room, built for Alice and Henry Young in 1899, is the largest room in the house. It has been the Museum's Trustees' Room and used for board meetings since 1937. It was restored in 1971, and retains all its original 1899 electric lighting fixtures and elaborate Tudor-style paneling. A reproduction brocade was put on the walls in 1971. The stained-glass skylight was restored as part of the 1994 project. Over the massive carved stone fireplace is a Latin inscription which, loosely translated, reads: "In all the earth, this corner smiles at me most."

THE YELLOW ROOM

THE GREEN ROOM

THE TRUSTEES' ROOM

The Preservation of
The Ballantine House

The Museum is only the third owner of the Ballantine House, and considering the changes that could have been made over time under institutional use, the alterations that were carried out between 1920 and 1975 were remarkably minimal. In 1975, exterior restoration was undertaken to remove ninety years' accumulation of dirt and carbon deposits that had blackened the brick and stonework. Long before the days of acid rain, Newark was a city full of factories, and those factories spewed coal smoke into the air day and night. For the Bicentennial project, the exterior of the house was thoroughly cleaned and the stonework restored wherever necessary. Where stone surfaces revealed minor or natural wear they were merely stabilized, but not restored. Actual restoration was necessary for almost fifty percent of the front porch's stonework, and involved the replacement of several of the delicately carved sandstone panels. After consulting original photographs and the existing decorative panels, craftsmen created plastic molds of missing flower and leaf designs and of the porch column capitals.

Newly molded sections were anchored to the original stone with expandable stainless steel to avoid future rusting or deterioration. To eliminate stress and weight problems, the new cornice panels were constructed of hollow fiberglass coated with a stone and resin mixture.

The exterior work required nine months to complete. In July 1975, the final scaffolding was removed and the restored exterior was once again on public view. The cost of the Bicentennial exterior restoration was generously financed by a City of Newark Capital Projects grant and private funds. Additional work to the exterior stonework was necessary for the 1994 project, due to water damage since 1976.

The 1994 project required more drastic measures than had been necessary in 1975. The massive slate-covered roof had begun to leak badly, and it was decided, as part of the environmental control for the entire building, that the roof needed to be entirely re-slated. In the course of preparation, it was discovered that a section of roof had been added in 1900, at the time of the building of Alice and Henry Young's library/living room, to link the new roofline with the old one. Beneath this addition a portion of the 1885 roof was entombed, untouched by weather or pollution. It became clear that the entire roof had already been replaced, either in 1900 for Alice Young, or in the 1920s by the insurance company. The entombed section of the roof provided samples of appropriate charcoal-gray slate for the new roof. Building Conservation Associates of New York City, and the John O'Hara Company of East Orange, worked together to recreate the lead-coated copper flashings and custom-made metalwork trim for the roof. Throughout the winter of 1993-1994—an especially harsh winter—scaffolding surrounded the house once again. An entirely new roof was built over the servants' wing and new mansard sheathing of dark slate gradually covered the century-old beams. As this went on outside, workers were busy inside as well.

ROOF REPLACEMENT, 1994

opposite page

The interior restoration of the second and third floors of the house was greatly complicated by the fact that the house needed to be climate controlled and to have entirely new fire suppression, security, and electrical systems. The steam heat system installed in 1900 was still in use, although it could not be calibrated with any precision. High fluctuation of heat during both winter and summer months was beginning to threaten the collections and the original architectural elements. In order to be a proper exhibition space for Museum collections, and indeed for the future preservation of its own irreplaceable woodwork and wall coverings, the house needed to be brought up to the environmental standards of the main Museum complex, completed in 1989. For a new building this is a fairly straightforward process, but for a century-old structure, and one that is a National Historic Landmark to boot, it was another story.

The climate control system consists of state-of-the-art mechanical equipment and various low-tech solutions. Building conservators determined the optimum climate range (temperature and humidity) that the house could tolerate without causing water condensation and deterioration within the brick walls. In conjunction with a complex heating-ventilation-air conditioning system (HVAC) with four separate zones, all the windows were removed and restored to make them airtight and waterproof. Interior storm windows of ultraviolet filtering glass, invisible from the outside, were designed to create an airlock and lessen heat and cold transfer through the large plate-glass windows. Because the first-floor period rooms were already restored, HVAC grills could not intrude into period surfaces, and thus the entire system had to be hidden within the 1885 walls. Fortunately, large gaps between the window casings, designed to hold the folded shutters, and the brick walls allowed for the ducting to be snaked through the first floor invisibly. On the second and third floors, where no period finishes had survived, large sections of plaster walls, ceilings, and pine flooring had to be taken out. Once all mechanical systems were installed, original floorboards were laid back in place, and plastering was redone, employing authentic Victorian methods. The original hardwood shutters are used in every window to control light and prevent ultraviolet damage to objects and painted finishes. The new roof itself was a major component of the climate control systems, and the old attic now houses modern machinery. The insurance company's coal cellar is now full of modern ductwork, which snakes all through the basement. The foundation was completely waterproofed to prevent dampness from affecting the climate within the house. The basement itself was left intact as much as possible, and the 1885 doors, brick walls, and hardware survive.

Along with the HVAC system, a sprinkler system was installed throughout the five levels of the house. Sprinkler heads were carefully placed to be as invisible as possible in the period rooms, and disguised with decorative paint to blend into the background colors. Smoke detectors and security system elements were also installed.

In the course of the complicated mechanical installation, much was learned about the construction of the house. It was an extremely well-built structure, which accounts in part for its survival. Floor joists were of 4 x 12-inch yellow pine planks—massively heavy—some of them as much as 20 feet long. Decorative floorboards were laid over up to eleven layers of rosin paper for soundproofing and to eliminate creaks. Between the floor joists, "pugging"—plaster and rubble with enough water to make them bind together—was used as fill to further soundproof the floors. This made the entire house extremely solid and heavy, and thus there was little settling and cracking of the walls over the following century. Ceilings were built not, like the walls, of traditional wood strips (lathe) with plaster, but of wire mesh with a thin coat of plaster. This allowed for lighter weight ceilings, which were less likely to crack. In 1885 this was a new technology, developed in England, and would have been costly.

As had been the case in the 1976 project on the first floor, the second-floor rooms had to be stripped of all modern fixtures. All the shutters were numbered, removed, and cleaned. Modern track lighting was added in the rooms to be used as galleries, and additional lighting was added to all the period rooms on both floors, to allow for easier visibility and reduction of overall light levels to protect the objects. Period fixtures use special 8.5-watt bulbs that imitate the look and brightness of a Victorian gas flame.

REPLACEMENT OF
SANDSTONE PANELS ON
FRONT PORCH, 1976

Conclusion

And so the Ballantine House stands, no longer a home, but recalling the time when it was a home. Today the great beer brewing family's mansion is open to everyone, free of charge, and in its period rooms, gallery rooms, and modern galleries people can explore, discover, and learn about what home meant a hundred years ago—and something of what it still means to many of us today. In its climate-controlled galleries, The Newark Museum's unique collection of domestic objects from four centuries is exhibited to encourage comparison and understanding. In its restored period rooms, objects of one era are placed in a rich visual context, giving them new life and new meaning for the modern visitor. Most important of all, one of this state's greatest architectural treasures has survived the changes in taste and fortune of a turbulent century in America, and will stand for the next generations—and the next millennium—as an eloquent testament to the American dream.